PRAISE FOR *YOUR AMAZING HANDS*

"A delightfully creative and insightful book that teaches our kids that Christianity is not just about behavior change but heart change too."

J.D. GREEAR, PASTOR, THE SUMMIT CHURCH

"The Training Young Hearts series is a favorite in our family. Abbey Wedgeworth packages big truths in bite-sized, understandable refrains that impact the hearts of children and their parents!"

GRETCHEN SAFFLES, WELL-WATERED WOMEN

"I trust Abbey's words and wisdom. I love thinking about these rich truths making their way into young hearts and minds."

DAVID THOMAS, AUTHOR, *RAISING EMOTIONALLY STRONG BOYS*

"Simplifying biblical truth for children takes a lot of hard work, and Abbey has done it creatively, faithfully, and accessibly. *Your Amazing Hands* will help children to see the wonderful gospel story—and help parents to see gospel opportunities in everyday situations."

JANE WATKINS, GROWING YOUNG DISCIPLES

"I adore how Abbey has brought her distinctive, gospel-centered encouragement and equipping to this series! *Your Amazing Hands* is a fun, engaging read that kids and caregivers will reach for often. They'll find themselves slowly shaped to use their hands in a way that esteems the way Christ used his hands—to save us and bring us to himself."

CAROLINE SAUNDERS, AUTHOR, *KIDS IN THE BIBLE*

Your Magnificent Mouth
© Abbey Wedgeworth 2025.

Illustrated by Emma Randall | Design & Art Direction by André Parker

Published in association with The Gates Group

"The Good Book For Children" is an imprint of The Good Book Company Ltd
North America: thegoodbook.com UK: thegoodbook.co.uk Australia: thegoodbook.com.au New Zealand: thegoodbook.co.nz India: thegoodbook.co.in

ISBN: 9781802541342 | JOB-007969 | Printed in India

Your mouth is **MAGNIFICENT!**
Your mouth can **SING!**
It can WHISPER and **SHOUT**
and say all sorts of things!

It's got **TEETH** that can chew...
LIPS to smack and to kiss...

CHEEKS to fill up with air...
   Your **TONGUE** tastes and it **CLICKS!**

Your mouth can **BLOW BUBBLES** and play the kazoo!

GOD'S magnificent mouth
made the whole **WORLD** with words!
Plants... oceans... stars... land...
fish, mammals, and birds!

It can comfort, encourage,
laugh, smile, and delight!
It can ask caring questions
or share great insights!

Yes, our mouths have great power!
They can do so much **MORE**!
But at times they do things
God did **NOT** make them for.

We might use them to lie,
    scream, be rude or unkind,
or say the worst things
    that come into our mind.

But God knew we'd mess up
with the mouths that he gave.
So he sent his Son, **JESUS,**
so we could be saved!

His mouth **ONLY** did
what God wanted it to.
He spoke words that were loving
and needed and true!

He made peace with his words.
His spit gave people sight.
He healed just by speaking!
He taught us what's right.

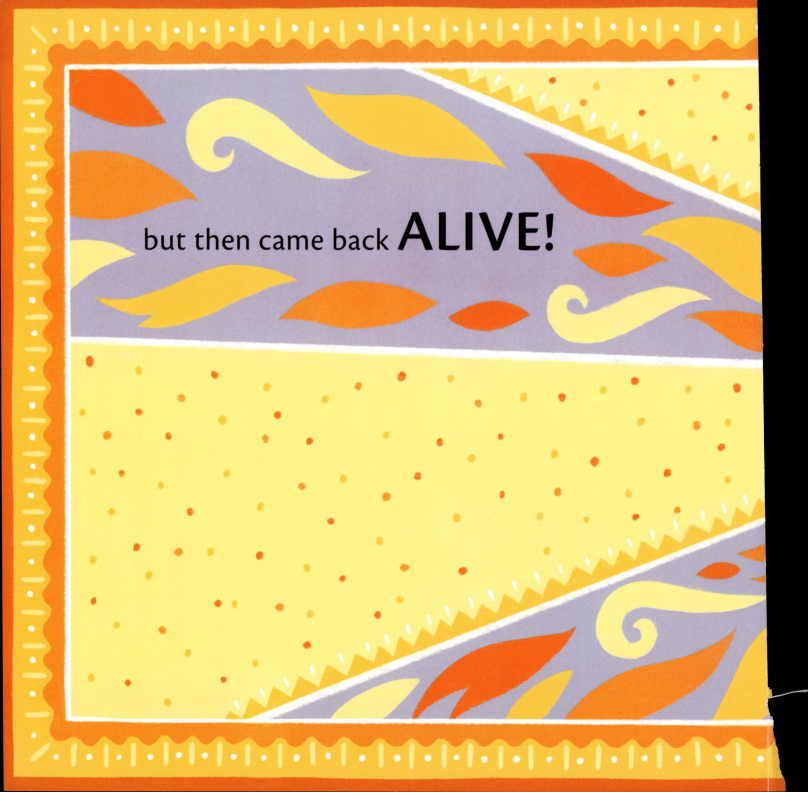
but then came back ALIVE!

And his mouth breathed the Spirit right onto his friends

to give them power to use their mouths for **GOOD** ends!

So when **YOUR** mouth blurts words
that aren't kind or aren't true,
and you feel icky inside,
here's some **GOOD NEWS** for you!

When you tell God,
"I'M SORRY!"
for the wrong that you've done,
you're forgiven, and helped
to be more like God's Son!

You're not on your own!
  Jesus' mouth prays for you!
All his friends get the power
  to do what God asks them to!

So when you are tempted,
you can pray right out loud!
"God, you made the whole world!
By your Spirit, help me now!"

Instead of making trouble,
    your words can make calm.
Instead of hurting or teasing,
    your words can heal like a balm.

What magnificent news!
Your mouth can tell
all your friends!

And sing and shout for Jesus, whose love and power **NEVER** end!

Follow Jesus' example and learn to rely on his amazing grace with
TRAINING YOUNG HEARTS

Rhyming books for ages 3+

Help children to see the goodness of the gospel as you celebrate God's plan for our incredible bodies—including the amazing truth that Jesus was perfect *for* us.

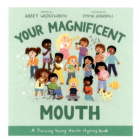

Lift-the-flap board books for toddlers

Simple, engaging, and practical, these books provide words to help you teach your kids about right and wrong actions, and point them to the gospel of grace.

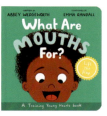

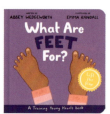

THEGOODBOOK.COM/TYH | THEGOODBOOK.CO.UK/TYH
THEGOODBOOK.COM.AU/TYH